AVFC
PREPARED

THE OFFICIAL
ASTON VILLA
ANNUAL 2013

Compiled by Rob Bishop and Ruth Pepler

A Grange Publication

© 2012. Published by Grange Communications Ltd., Edinburgh, under licence from Aston Villa Football Club. Printed in the EU.

Special thanks to Gayner Monkton, Lorna McClelland and John Devlin

Photographs © Neville Williams and Getty Images

ISBN: 978-1-908925-01-5

£7.99

CLUB
HONOURS

European Cup
Winners: 1981-82
Quarter-finalists: 1982-83

European Super Cup
Winners: 1982-83

World Clubs Championship
Runners-up: 1982

Intertoto Cup
Winners: 2001

Football League
Champions: 1893-94, 1895-96, 1896-97,
1898-99, 1899-1900, 1909-10, 1980-81
Runners-up: 1888-89, 1902-03,
1907-08, 1910-11, 1912-13, 1913-14,
1930-31, 1932-33, 1989-90

Premier League
Runners-up: 1992-93

Division Two
Champions: 1937-38, 1959-60

Division Three
Champions: 1971-72

FA Cup
Winners: 1887, 1895, 1897, 1905, 1913,
1920, 1957
Runners-up: 1892, 1924, 2000

League Cup
Winners: 1961, 1975, 1977, 1994, 1996
Runners-up: 1963, 1971, 2010

FA Youth Cup
Winners: 1972, 1980, 2002
Runners-up: 1978, 2004, 2010

CONTENTS

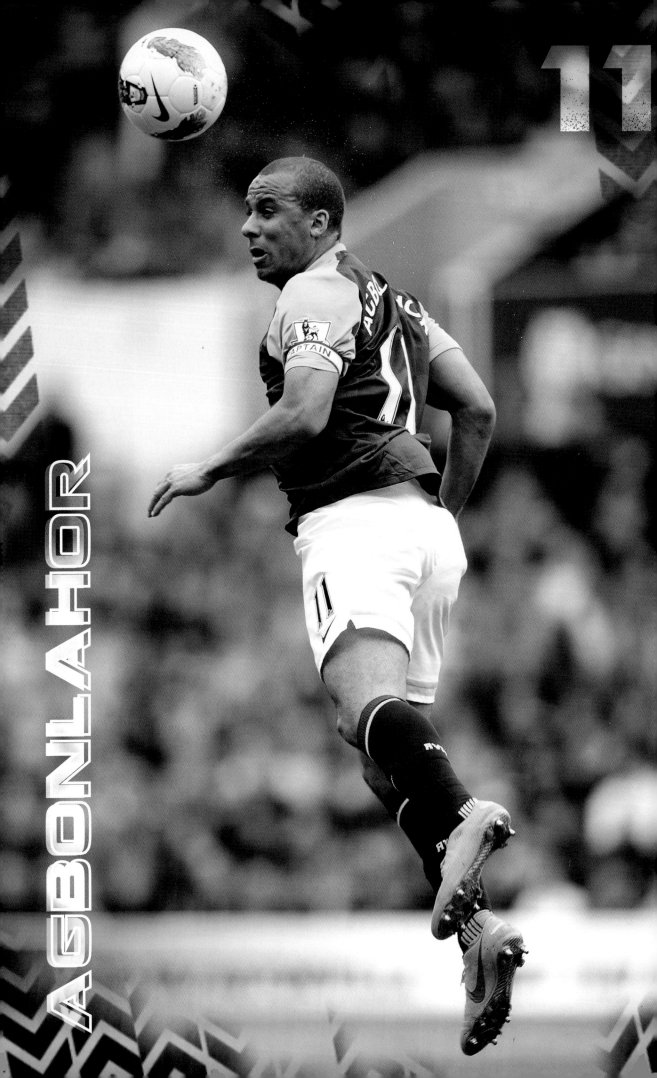

IT'S A DEAL

But we will have to wait...

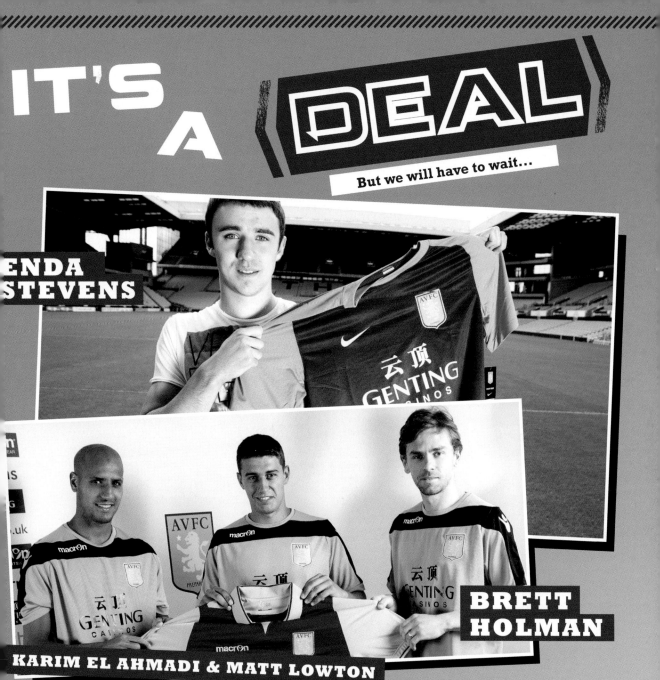

ENDA STEVENS

KARIM EL AHMADI & MATT LOWTON

BRETT HOLMAN

Football transfers sometimes take quite a while to come to fruition – and in some cases they can take several months!

When Enda Stevens arrived at Villa last January, for instance, the Irish full-back had actually agreed to join the club the previous summer.

And it was a similar situation when Brett Holman became a Villan at the start of the season. The deal for the Australian forward had been negotiated in March!

What happed in both cases is that the players signed what is known as a pre-contract agreement. They committed their futures to

Villa – but not until they had honoured the contracts with their previous clubs.

So Enda continued to play for Irish club Shamrock Rovers until the New Year, gaining vital experience in the group stages of the UEFA Europa League, while Brett completed the season with Dutch club AZ Alkmaar.

Both players have won honours with their previous clubs, Enda enjoying League of Ireland titles with Shamrock in 2010 and 2011 and Brett helping Alkmaar to the Dutch championship and Super Cup in 2009.

Here's hoping they add to their medal collections in claret and blue...

SLEEPING ON THE BALL!

Z Z Z Z Z Z

No doubt you've heard of someone who eats, drinks and sleeps football? What it means, of course, is that you are totally devoted to the game.

That's certainly the case for Karim El Ahmadi. And while we are sure he has never actually attempted to eat a ball, he has certainly slept with one!

The 27-year-old former Feyenoord midfielder took his football everywhere with him when he was a boy – even when he went to bed. "When I was young I was always playing on the streets with the ball," he said. "We didn't have any PlayStations or anything like that, so the ball was everything for me. I was sleeping with the ball and when I went shopping with my mum I would take it with me."

Now the Dutch-born Morocco international is encouraging his nephews to be just as devoted.

"They are good players, but I've told them they have to be mentally sure that they want to be football players," he said. "At the time when I was young it was only the ball that I wanted. Now I see with my nephews that it's also the computers. When I tell them to go and play with the ball, they want to play with the PlayStation!"

Karim's time on the ball during his formative years has certainly paid off. Having started his professional career with Twente in his home town Enschede, he joined Feyenoord in 2008.

RON'S REQUESTS

The ink had barely dried on Ron Vlaar's contract when he proved just how committed he is to the claret and blue cause.

Within minutes of signing for Villa from Feyenoord, the 27-year-old Dutch defender made two requests:

> 1- Can I get a subscription to AVTV?
> 2- I want to meet Villa supporters!

Ron's transfer was completed on the day Villa played at Peterborough in a pre-season friendly, so he was anxious to take a look at his new team-mates in action via the club's official online TV channel.

And his request to meet the fans was granted a couple of days later when arrangements were made for a signing session at the Villa Store.

"I hope my relationship with the Villa fans becomes the same as my relationship with Feyenoord's fans," he said. "I was seven years at Feyenoord and the fans were great with me. In my opinion, the fans and the players have to work together to make everything better and get the right results. We have to do it on the pitch and they have to support us in the stands."

Ron, who played two games for Holland in last summer's European Championship finals, is also aiming to emulate some of the club's top centre-backs.

"I am looking forward to following in the footsteps of players like Paul McGrath, Olof Mellberg and Martin Laursen," he said. "But I also do things for myself because I want to get the very best out of myself. I can't do that alone. I also need the other players in the team."

HUNGARY TO LEARN

He was born in Derbyshire and has played most of his games just up the road in South Yorkshire. But Matthew Lowton travelled nearly 1,000 miles for one of the most vital parts of his football education.

In 2009, the full-back left Sheffield United for a loan spell with Hungarian club Ferencvaros and learned a lot while he was in Budapest. "I was playing reserve football a lot of the time and the gaffer at the time sent me over there to play first team football," he said.

"I moved out there when I was 17. I had to live on my own, fend for myself and then play first team football. So it definitely helped me grow up, get used to first team games and bigger crowds. It definitely helped me and is probably why I am where I am now."

Having played 18 times for Ferencvaros – and helped them to gain promotion back to the Hungarian top flight - Matthew returned to Bramall Lane and went on to break into the Blades' first team.

He played in every game for them last season, and was in the team who suffered heartache at the hands of Huddersfield Town in the League One play-off final at Wembley.

His impressive form caught the eye of Paul Lambert, who had no hesitation in signing Matthew after becoming Villa's new boss. It's quite a leap from League One to the Premier League, but Matthew is determined to adapt.

"I was overwhelmed the first time I saw the training ground," he said. "The players in the dressing room, the manager, everything is higher profile and it just seems surreal.

"It was daunting, it was fantastic to even meet players like the lads here, but now I've got the chance to play with them."

"IT DEFINITELY HELPED ME AND IS PROBABLY WHY I AM WHERE I AM NOW"

VILLA STARS

★ SHAY GIVEN ★

Born: LIFFORD, IRELAND, 20/04/1976
Position: GOALKEEPER
Joined Villa: JULY 2011
Debut: FULHAM (A) 13/08/2011
Previous clubs:
NEWCASTLE UNITED, MANCHESTER CITY

2011-12 record:
APPEARANCES – 32 league, 2 cup

★ MATTHEW LOWTON ★

Born: CHESTERFIELD, 09/06/1989
Position: DEFENDER
Joined Villa: JULY 2012
Previous clubs: SHEFFIELD UNITED,
FERENCVAROS (loan)

★ BRETT HOLMAN ★

Born: SYDNEY, AUSTRALIA, 27/03/1984
Position: STRIKER
Joined Villa: JULY 2012
Previous clubs: FEYENOORD, EXCELSIOR,
NEC NIJMEGEN, AZ ALKMAAR

KARIM EL AHMADI

Born: ENSCHEDE, HOLLAND, 27/01/1985
Position: MIDFIELDER
Joined Villa: JULY 2012
Previous clubs: TWENTE, FEYENOORD

RICHARD DUNNE

Born: DUBLIN, IRELAND, 21/09/1979
Position: CENTRAL DEFENDER
Signed for Villa: AUGUST 2009
Debut: BIRMINGHAM CITY (A) 13/09/2009
Previous clubs: EVERTON,
MANCHESTER CITY

2011-12 record:
APPEARANCES – 28 league, 4 cup
GOALS – 1 league, 1 cup

BRAD GUZAN

Born: CHICAGO, USA, 09/09/1984
Position: GOALKEEPER
Signed for Villa: AUGUST 2008
Debut: QPR (H) CARLING CUP 24/09/2008
Previous clubs: CHIVAS USA

2011-12 record:
APPEARANCES – 6 (1 sub) league, 2 cup

★ CIARAN CLARK ★

Born: HARROW, 26/09/1989
Position: CENTRAL DEFENDER
Debut: FULHAM (H) 30/08/2009
Previous clubs: NONE

2011-12 record:
APPEARANCES – 13 (2 sub) league, 3 cup
GOALS – 1 league, 1 cup

★ RON VLAAR ★

Born: HENSBROEK, HOLLAND, 16/02/1985
Position: DEFENDER
Joined Villa: AUGUST 2012
Previous clubs: AZ ALKMAAR, FEYENOORD

★ ERIC LICHAJ ★

Born: CHICAGO, USA, 17/11/1988
Position: FULL-BACK
Debut: RAPID VIENNA (A) EUROPA LEAGUE, 19/08/2010
Previous clubs: NONE

2011-12 record:
APPEARANCES - 9 (1 sub) league, 1 cup
GOALS - 1 league, 1 cup

★ NATHAN BAKER ★

Born: WORCESTER, 23/04/1991
Position: FULL-BACK
Debut: WIGAN ATHLETIC (A) 25/01/2011
Previous clubs: NONE

2011-12 record:
APPEARANCES - 6 (2 sub) league

★ ENDA STEVENS ★

Born: DUBLIN, IRELAND, 09/07/1990
Position: FULL-BACK
Joined Villa: JANUARY 2012
Previous club: SHAMROCK ROVERS

★ STILIYAN PETROV ★

Born: MONTANA, BULGARIA, 05/07/1979
Position: MIDFIELDER
Signed for Villa: AUGUST 2006
Debut: WEST HAM (A) 10/09/2006
Previous clubs: CSKA SOFIA, CELTIC

2011-12 record:
APPEARANCES - 26 (1 sub) league, 3 cup
GOALS - 4 league

FABIAN DELPH

Born: BRADFORD, 21/11/1989
Position: MIDFIELDER
Signed for Villa: AUGUST 2009
Debut: WIGAN ATHLETIC (H), 15/08/2009
Previous club: LEEDS UNITED

2011-12 record:
APPEARANCES – 10 (1 sub) league

MARC ALBRIGHTON

Born: TAMWORTH, 18/11/1989
Position: MIDFIELDER
Debut: CSKA MOSCOW (A) UEFA CUP,
26/02/2009
Previous clubs: NONE

2011-12 record:
APPEARANCES – 15 (11 sub) league, 3 cup
GOALS – 2 league, 1 cup

JEAN II MAKOUN

Born: YAOUNDÉ, CAMEROON, 29/05/1983
Position: MIDFIELDER
Signed for Villa: JANUARY 2011
Debut: WIGAN ATHLETIC (A) 25/01/2011
Previous clubs: LILLE OSC,
OLYMPIQUE LYONNAIS

2011-12 record:
APPEARANCES – 1 cup

★ BARRY BANNAN ★

Born: GLASGOW, 01/12/1989
Position: MIDFIELDER
Debut: HAMBURG (A) UEFA CUP,
17/12/2008
Previous clubs: NONE

2011-12 record:
APPEARANCES – 10 (18 sub) league,
2 (2 sub) cup
GOALS – 1 league

★ CHARLES N'ZOGBIA ★

Born: HARFLEUR, FRANCE, 28/05/1986
Position: MIDFIELDER
Signed for Villa: JULY 2011
Debut: FULHAM (A) 13/08/2011
Previous clubs: LE HAVRE, NEWCASTLE
UNITED, WIGAN ATHLETIC

2011-12 record:
APPEARANCES – 24 (6 sub) league,
1 (1 sub) cup
GOALS – 2 league

★ GARY GARDNER ★

Born: SOLIHULL, 26/02/1992
Position: MIDFIELDER
Debut: CHELSEA (A) 31/12/2011
Previous clubs: NONE

2011-12 record:
APPEARANCES – 5 (9 sub) league,
0 (2 sub) cup

★ DARREN BENT ★

Born: LONDON, 06/02/1984
Position: STRIKER
Signed for Villa: JANUARY 2011
Debut: MANCHESTER CITY (H) 22/01/2011
Previous clubs: IPSWICH TOWN,
CHARLTON ATHLETIC, TOTTENHAM
HOTSPUR, SUNDERLAND

2011-12 record:
APPEARANCES - 21 (1 sub) league, 3 cup
GOALS - 9 league, 1 cup

★ GABRIEL AGBONLAHOR ★

Born: BIRMINGHAM, 13/10/1986
Position: STRIKER
Debut: EVERTON (A) 18/03/2006
Previous clubs: NONE

2011-12 record:
APPEARANCES - 32 (1 sub) league,
2 (1 sub) cup
GOALS - 5 league, 1 cup

★ NATHAN DELFOUNESO ★

Born: BIRMINGHAM, 02/02/1991
Position: STRIKER
Signed professional: FEBRUARY 2008
Debut: HAFNARFJORDUR (A) UEFA CUP,
14/08/08
Previous clubs: NONE

2011-12 record:
APPEARANCES - 1 (5 sub) league,
1 (1 sub) cup
GOALS - 1 cup

★ ANDREAS WEIMANN ★

  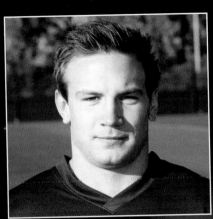

Born: VIENNA, AUSTRIA, 05/08/1991
Position: STRIKER
Signed: AUGUST 2008
Debut: WEST HAM (H) 14/08/2010
Previous clubs: NONE

2011-12 record:
APPEARANCES – 5 (9 sub) league,
0 (1 sub) cup
GOALS – 2 league

★ CHRIS HERD ★

Born: MELBOURNE, AUSTRALIA, 04/04/1989
Position: MIDFIELDER or DEFENDER
Debut: MANCHESTER UNITED (H),
13/11/2010
Previous clubs: NONE

2011-12 record:
APPEARANCES – 19 league, 1 cup
GOALS – 1 league

★ SAMIR CARRUTHERS ★

Born: LONDON, 04/04/1993
Position: MIDFIELDER
Debut: LIVERPOOL (A) 07/04/2012
Previous clubs: NONE

2011-12 record:
APPEARANCES – 0 (3 sub) league

Q & A with
GARY GARDNER

Midfielder Gary Gardner is the youngest of six brothers whose football loyalties are divided. For Gary, though, there's only one team and that's Villa.

Can you remember your first visit to Villa Park?

It was to watch my older brother Craig playing in a cup final for his school team, so I was very young - maybe only seven. One of the first Villa games I remember was when we beat Coventry City in the last home match of the 2000-01 season. Mustapha Hadji scored twice for Coventry in the first half but Villa hit back to win 3-2 with goals from Darius Vassell, Juan Pablo Angel and Paul Merson.

What was your first Villa replica kit?

I had a lot of kits, to be fair; not just Villa but other Premier League clubs, too, and even some Spanish ones. But the first Villa shirt I remember wearing was the striped one when LDV Vans were the sponsors.

You joined Villa's Academy at the age of seven. How did that come about?

I was spotted playing for my Sunday League Olton Ravens team and was asked if I wanted to train at Bodymoor Heath. I did that for about a year and then signed when I was eight - and started playing for Villa's Under-9s. That was before Craig joined. I always remind him that I was with Villa before he was!

Who was your boyhood hero?

Although I'm a Villa supporter, the player I admired most as a kid was Liverpool's Steven Gerrard. He's the player I've tried to emulate in terms of the way he plays. I also loved watching Gareth Barry in action for Villa.

It must have helped, having your big brother at the club?

Definitely. Watching him progress to the first team helped me appreciate what it takes to be a Premier League footballer. Neither of us drinks alcohol, that's the way our mum and dad brought us up. There are six brothers altogether - three of us support Villa, the other three follow Blues. We always had season tickets at both grounds, and we all went to a game every week. It cost our dad a fortune!

Villa fans obviously know Craig. Tell us about your other brothers.

Every one of them has played football at some stage. Craig and I made it as professionals but the other lads could play a bit, as well. Richard had a trial with Walsall, Mark was at Solihull Moors, Terry was at Tamworth and Carl was also a keen player. We're a football family.

What honours have you won?

I helped Villa to win the FA Premier Reserve League in 2009. We won the Southern section and then beat Northern champions Sunderland in the final. I went on as a sub in that game.

What's the highlight of your career so far?

There are three of them, really. Making my first team debut as a sub in a 3-1 win at Chelsea was special, and being in the starting line-up when we won 3-2 away to Wolves was great as well. But the game which really stands out is my home debut against Manchester City. We lost 1-0 but stepping out in front of a big crowd at Villa Park was what I'd dreamed of when I was a young lad.

How much does it mean to you to be a Villa player?

It's a massive thing for me. I sometimes have to pinch myself because it was what I wanted from a very young age.

What advice would you give to youngsters wanting to be professional footballers?

Keep working hard and stay away from alcohol. Never give up - if you want something badly enough you will get it.

AUGUST

Summary signings Shay Given and Charles N'Zogbia make their debuts on the opening day of the season, helping Villa to a goalless draw against Fulham at Craven Cottage.

That promising start is followed by a 3-1 victory over Blackburn Rovers in the first Villa Park game of the new campaign. Gabby Agbonlahor scores Villa's first competitive goal of the season – his 50th in the Premier League – with Emile Heskey and Darren Bent also on target against the Ewood Park outfit.

There's also a goalless draw against Wolves at Villa Park, while Villa beat Hereford United 2-0 in the second round of the Carling Cup.

The Bulls provide stern resistance to Alex McLeish's men but Eric Lichaj breaks the deadlock with his first Villa goal and Nathan Delfouneso quickly follows up with a second.

The club make two signings on transfer deadline day. Right-back Alan Hutton signs from Tottenham Hotspur on a four-year contract, while midfielder Jermaine Jenas arrives on a season-long loan from the White Hart Lane club.

Both players make a late-night appearance under the floodlights at a deserted Villa Park as they are interviewed by AVTV.

AT A GLANCE

DATE	OPPONENTS	V	RESULT	SCORERS
AUG 13	FULHAM	A	0-0	
AUG 20	BLACKBURN ROVERS	H	3-1	AGBONLAHOR, BENT, HESKEY
AUG 23	HEREFORD UNITED (CC)	H	2-0	LICHAJ, DELFOUNESO
AUG 27	WOLVES	H	0-0	

Despite trailing twice at Goodison Park, Villa hit back to draw 2-2 with Everton, thanks to fine equalisers from Stiliyan Petrov and Gabby Agbonlahor.

The skipper is on target with a superb dipping 25-yard shot which flies into the corner of the net, with Gabby heading home Marc Albrighton's left-wing cross in the closing minutes.

Agbonlahor is also on target to give Villa an interval lead at home to in-form Newcastle United, although the Magpies hit back with a second-half equaliser to sneak away with a point.

Watched by David Cameron at Loftus Road the following Sunday, Villa delight the Prime Minister by taking the lead with a penalty from Barry Bannan, only to concede a late equaliser in a 1-1 draw against newly-promoted Queens Park Rangers.

The result in west London means the boys in claret and blue are still unbeaten in the Barclays Premier League after six games, although any hopes of an extended run in the Carling Cup are extinguished by a 2-0 home defeat at the hands of Bolton Wanderers in round three.

AT A GLANCE

DATE	OPPONENTS	V	RESULT	SCORERS
SEPT 10	EVERTON	A	2-2	PETROV, AGBONLAHOR
SEPT 17	NEWCASTLE UTD	H	1-1	AGBONLAHOR
SEPT 20	BOLTON WANDERERS (CC)	H	0-2	
SEPT 25	QPR	A	1-1	BANNAN (PEN)

They say good things are always worth waiting for – and that is certainly the case when Villa beat Wigan Athletic 2-0 at home on the first Saturday of October.

It's the first time we have recorded a home win over the Latics since their promotion to the top flight in 2005 – and England international Darren Bent is on target at the Holte End for the first time since his record transfer from Sunderland. Bent's second-half goal clinches victory after Villa lead through Gabby Agbonlahor at the interval.

There's another significant moment the following week when left-back Stephen

Warnock scores his first league goal for the club. But he's not in the mood for celebrating – his goal comes in a 4-1 defeat by Manchester City at the Etihad Stadium.

Chris Herd is controversially sent off in a 2-1 home defeat by West Bromwich Albion after Darren Bent opens the scoring from the penalty spot. The red card is rescinded a few days later.

Stiliyan Petrov, meanwhile, marks his 200th Villa appearance by hitting the first goal in a 2-2 draw against Sunderland, with Richard Dunne also on target at the Stadium of Light.

AT A GLANCE

DATE	OPPONENTS	V	RESULT	SCORERS
OCT 1	WIGAN ATHLETIC	H	2-0	AGBONLAHOR, BENT
OCT 15	MANCHESTER CITY	A	1-4	WARNOCK
OCT 22	WEST BROMWICH ALBION	H	1-2	BENT (PEN)
OCT 29	SUNDERLAND	A	2-2	PETROV, DUNNE

Darren Bent scores twice as Villa beat Norwich City 3-2 – with both his goals set up by Gabby Agbonlahor.

And with Gabby also on target in an exciting, entertaining contest it's no great surprise that his super show earns him a recall to the England squad. But football is never quite that simple, and he is forced to withdraw from international duty because of a hamstring problem.

After the game against the Canaries, Villa have an extended break before their next action – and the team suffer for their inactivity.

They never get going against Tottenham Hotspur at White Hart Lane, suffering a 2-0 defeat which is far more emphatic than the score-line suggests. There's a sombre mood at the Liberty Stadium on the final Sunday of the month as players from both Swansea City and Villa come to terms with the death of Wales manager Gary Speed ahead of a goalless draw.

Plenty of Villa players are on the move, with Habib Beye, Gary Gardner, Shane Lowry and Nathan Baker all going out on loan to Championship clubs. Beye joins Doncaster Rovers, Gardner links up with Coventry City, and Lowry and Baker both move to Millwall.

AT A GLANCE

DATE	OPPONENTS	V	RESULT	SCORERS
NOV 5	NORWICH CITY	H	3-2	BENT 2, AGBONLAHOR
NOV 21	TOTTENHAM HOTSPUR	A	0-2	
NOV 27	SWANSEA CITY	A	0-0	

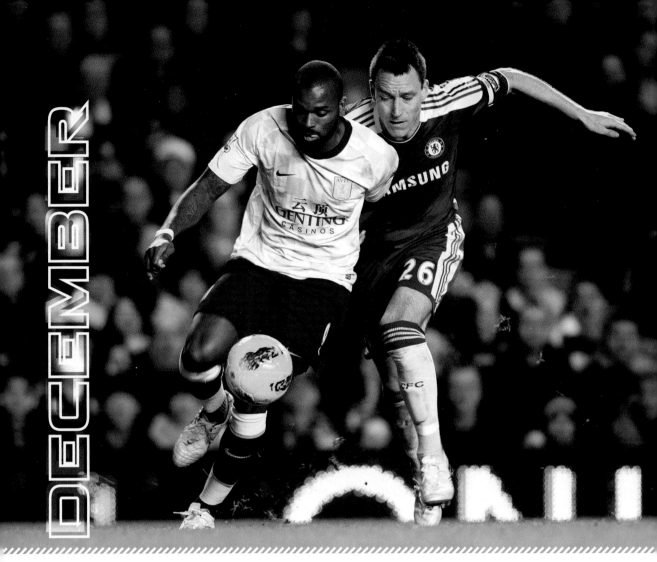

Former England international Emile Heskey reaches a significant milestone, making his 500th Premier League appearance when he goes on as a 63rd minute substitute for Jermaine Jenas in the home game against Manchester United. But it's not an occasion to remember as Villa lose 1-0.

There's a happier scenario the following Saturday as Marc Albrighton scores his first goal of the season to set up Villa's first away win of 2011-12, a 2-1 success over Bolton at the Reebok Stadium. Stiliyan Petrov is also on target with a shot which takes a slight deflection off former Villa defender Zat Knight.

Albrighton's 54th-minute equaliser against Arsenal is the 20,000th goal to be scored in the Premier League since its inception in 1992. Unfortunately, the game ends in a 2-1 defeat just three days after Liverpool win 2-0 at Villa Park.

After a goalless draw against Stoke City at the Britannia Stadium on Boxing Day, Villa sign off 2011 in style with a 3-1 victory over Chelsea at Stamford Bridge. Stephen Ireland equalises to cancel out a Didier Drogba penalty, with Petrov and Darren Bent completing an excellent win with goals in the last 10 minutes.

AT A GLANCE

DATE	OPPONENTS	V	RESULT	SCORERS
DEC 3	MANCHESTER UNITED	H	0-1	
DEC 10	BOLTON WANDERERS	A	2-1	ALBRIGHTON, PETROV
DEC 18	LIVERPOOL	H	0-2	
DEC 21	ARSENAL	H	1-2	ALBRIGHTON
DEC 26	STOKE CITY	A	0-0	
DEC 31	CHELSEA	A	3-1	IRELAND, PETROV, BENT

Sometimes there's just no logic in football. Just 48 hours after seeing out 2011 with a Stamford Bridge super show, Villa can do nothing right in their New Year Bank Holiday clash with Swansea City, slipping to a 2-0 home defeat.

The first hurdle of the FA Cup is safely negotiated – a 3-1 win away to Bristol Rovers, thanks to Marc Albrighton, Gabby Agbonlahor and a superb Ciaran Clark effort – only for the team to fall at the second fence. Two-up at half-time through Richard Dunne and Darren Bent, they eventually lose 3-2 to Arsenal in a fourth round tie at the Emirates Stadium.

Irish full-back Enda Stevens joins the club from Shamrock Rovers and there's another new Irishman in the ranks as Robbie Keane arrives on a six-week loan from LA Galaxy.

The Republic's leading scorer makes his debut as a substitute in a 1-1 home draw against Everton – and a week later he is on target twice against the club where he started his career. Villa emerge 3-2 winners over Wolves at Molineux, taking the lead with a Darren Bent penalty and then trailing 2-1 at half-time before Keane clinches maximum points with two stunning second half strikes.

AT A GLANCE

DATE	OPPONENTS	V	RESULT	SCORERS
JAN 2	SWANSEA CITY	H	0-2	
JAN 7	BRISTOL ROVERS (FAC3)	A	3-1	ALBRIGHTON, AGBONLAHOR, CLARK
JAN 14	EVERTON	H	1-1	BENT
JAN 21	WOLVES	A	3-2	BENT (PEN), KEANE 2
JAN 29	ARSENAL (FAC4)	A	2-3	DUNNE, BENT

There's a very special moment for Darren Bent as he scores his 100th Premier League goal – and it couldn't be more timely. Villa are trailing 2-0 at home to Queens Park Rangers when the England striker converts Alan Hutton's low centre to spark a comeback.

Charles N'Zogbia's second-half equaliser – his first goal since his transfer from Wigan Athletic the previous summer – ensures a point in a 2-2 draw.

Robbie Keane's goal isn't enough to prevent a 2-1 defeat at Newcastle, and there's also a 1-0 home defeat at the hands of Manchester City, whose goal is scored by Villa fan Joleon Lescott. The City game is particularly painful for Richard Dunne, who suffers a fractured shoulder against his former club.

Keane makes his final appearance in a goalless draw against Wigan Athletic before heading back across the Atlantic to re-join American club LA Galaxy – and there's even more depressing news for Darren Bent.

The striker suffers a serious ankle injury at the DW Stadium and is ruled out for the rest of the season.

AT A GLANCE

DATE	OPPONENTS	V	RESULT	SCORERS
FEB 1	QUEENS PARK RANGERS	H	2-2	BENT, N'ZOGBIA
FEB 5	NEWCASTLE UNITED	A	1-2	KEANE
FEB 12	MANCHESTER CITY	H	0-1	
FEB 25	WIGAN ATHLETIC	A	0-0	

It's very much a case of Handy Andi as Andreas Weimann scores his first senior goal and Villa end a run of six games without a win. The home match against Fulham is heading towards a goalless draw when three substitutes combine to clinch a dramatic victory in stoppage time.

Barry Bannan's pass across the penalty area sets up Gary Gardner for a stinging shot which is too hot for Mark Schwarzer to hold. And although Fulham's keeper pushes out Andreas Weimann's diving header from the rebound, the young Austrian manages to scramble the ball over the line with his knee. It's a wonderful moment for Andreas in front of the Holte End, and a relief to Villa's players and supporters, who celebrate the 1-0 win as if we have won the FA Cup.

The Fulham finale, sadly, is the only real highlight of an otherwise depressing month. Charles N'Zogbia opens the scoring against Blackburn Rovers with a fine goal at Ewood Park, only for the home side to grab a late equaliser, and is followed by two defeats, 3-0 at Arsenal and 4-2 to Chelsea. Worse still is the news that skipper Stiliyan Petrov has been diagnosed with acute leukaemia. The Bulgarian midfielder's presence at the Chelsea game inspires Villa to hit back from two-down with goals from James Collins and Eric Lichaj before Villa run out of steam.

AT A GLANCE

DATE	OPPONENTS	V	RESULT	SCORERS
MAR 3	BLACKBURN ROVERS	A	1-1	N'ZOGBIA
MAR 10	FULHAM	H	1-0	WEIMANN
MAR 24	ARSENAL	A	0-3	
MAR 31	CHELSEA	H	2-4	COLLINS, LICHAJ

This month is the wettest April on record – and there few bright periods for Villa as they continue to be the Premier League's draw specialists.

The highlight is undoubtedly a 1-1 draw at Liverpool, where Australian Chris Herd scores his first goal for the club at Anfield's famous Kop end. It's a superb shot into the top corner following a fine pass from Barry Bannan – though Andreas Weimann's goal in a 1-1 home draw against Stoke City is even more impressive.

Accepting Eric Lichaj's pass from the left touchline, the Austrian striker exchanges passes with Stephen Ireland before curling a perfect right-foot shot into the far corner from the edge of the penalty area.

After a 4-0 defeat by Manchester United at Old Trafford, Villa draw 0-0 at home to Sunderland, and despite taking the lead through Stephen Warnock, the team concede two goals in as many minutes to lose 2-1 at home to Bolton Wanderers.

But there's a ray of sunshine in the derby against West Bromwich Albion at The Hawthorns, Richard Dunne returning to action and helping Villa to take a hard-earned point from a goalless draw.

AT A GLANCE

DATE	OPPONENTS	V	RESULT	SCORERS
APR 7	LIVERPOOL	A	1-1	HERD
APR 9	STOKE CITY	H	1-1	WEIMANN
APR 15	MANCHESTER UNITED	A	0-4	
APR 21	SUNDERLAND	H	0-0	
APR 24	BOLTON WANDERERS	H	1-2	WARNOCK
APR 28	WEST BROMWICH ALBION	A	0-0	

For only the third time since the launch of the Premier League, Villa find themselves battling for top-flight survival going into the last couple of games of the season.

There's certainly a tense atmosphere for the final home match as Tottenham Hotspur arrive at Villa Park in pursuit of Champions League qualification, although Ciaran Clark settles Villa's nerves with a 30-yard shot which hits William Gallas and loops over keeper Brad Friedel to open the scoring in the 35th minute.

The Londoners are reduced to 10 men early in the second half when Danny Rose is sent off but that seems to galvanise Harry Redknapp's men, who equalise with a penalty from Emmanuel Adebayor.

Even so, Villa's point in a 1-1 draw effectively secures the club's 21st consecutive season of Premier League football.

If that brings a huge sigh of relief, though, there's no happy end to the 2011-12 campaign. Alex McLeish's side are outplayed in a 2-0 defeat by Norwich City at Carrow Road and less than 24 hours later the manager is sacked after just 11 months in charge.

AT A GLANCE

DATE	OPPONENTS	V	RESULT	SCORERS
MAY 6	TOTTENHAM HOTSPUR	H	1-1	CLARK
MAY 13	NORWICH CITY	A	0-2	

		P	W	D	L	F	A	GD	PTS
1	Manchester City	38	28	5	5	93	29	+64	89
2	Manchester United	38	28	5	5	89	33	+56	89
3	Arsenal	38	21	7	10	74	49	+25	70
4	Tottenham Hotspur	38	20	9	9	66	41	+25	69
5	Newcastle United	38	19	8	11	56	51	+5	65
6	Chelsea	38	18	10	10	65	46	+19	64
7	Everton	38	15	11	12	50	40	+10	56
8	Liverpool	38	14	10	14	47	40	+7	52
9	Fulham	38	14	10	14	48	51	-3	52
10	WB Albion	38	13	8	17	45	52	-7	47
11	Swansea City	38	12	11	15	44	51	-7	47
12	Norwich City	38	12	11	15	52	66	-14	47
13	Sunderland	38	11	12	15	45	46	-1	45
14	Stoke City	38	11	12	15	36	53	-17	45
15	Wigan Athletic	38	11	10	17	42	62	-20	43
16	Aston Villa	38	7	17	14	37	53	-16	38
17	Queens Park Rangers	38	10	7	21	43	66	-23	37
18	Bolton Wanderers	38	10	6	22	46	77	-31	36
19	Blackburn Rovers	38	8	7	23	48	78	-30	31
20	Wolverhampton W.	38	5	10	23	40	82	-42	25

FACTS AND FIGURES

- League position - 16th
- FA Cup - Round 4
- Carling Cup - Round 3
- Leading scorer - Darren Bent (10)
- Most league appearances -
  Stephen Warnock (34 plus 1 sub)
- Biggest win - 3-1 v Blackburn Rovers (h)
  and Chelsea (a)
- Heaviest defeat -
  4-0 v Manchester United (a)
- Highest home attendance -
  40,055 v Manchester United
- Average home attendance - 33,873

DEBUTS

Shay Given v Fulham (a)

Charles N'Zogbia v Fulham (a)

Alan Hutton v Everton (a)

Jermaine Jenas v Norwich City (h)

Gary Gardner v Chelsea (a)

Robbie Keane v Everton (h)

Samir Carruthers v Liverpool (a)

GIVEN

1

MORE THAN A GAME

There's more to football than 90 minutes' action on the pitch, as these offbeat stories illustrate…

ANDI ON HIS MARKS

Andreas Weimann is used to being interviewed for football publications so it made a welcome change when he was featured in an athletics magazine.

Athletics Weekly sent along a reporter to the Bodymoor Heath training ground to talk to Andi about his parents Sabine and Thomas, who were both Austrian sprint hurdles champions.

"It's the first time I've been interviewed by an athletics magazine," he said. "But it made a nice change from talking about football!"

·DARREN ON CORRIE·

You wouldn't normally expect to hear a Villa player mentioned in top soap Coronation Street, where the footie talk normally focuses on the Manchester clubs and the fictitious Weatherfield Town.

But it happened during a Corrie conversation between Tommy, Tyrone and Tina. This is how it went

Tommy (to Tyrone): *You need your head examining.*
Tina: *What's going on?*
Tyrone: *Nowt.*
Tina: *Why does he need his head examining?*
Tommy: *Fantasy football. He thinks Darren Bent's going to be top scorer.*

Needless to say, Darren was flattered to get a mention. As a London lad, though, he prefers Eastenders!

FIFA STREET FUN

Villa quartet Darren Bent, Ciaran Clark, Gary Gardner and Barry Bannan were involved in a different kind of football when they tried out the new FIFA Street game – with Gary and Barry emerging victorious.

ONE SHOT ON TARGET?

There's a new blockbuster film due out this winter – and it might well feature a character with claret and blue connections.

Thriller writer Lee Child's book *One Shot* is being made into a movie starring Tom Cruise, who will be playing the part of hero Jack Reacher.

Even though they are based in America, many of Lee Child's books include Villa names, with Paul McGrath, Milosevic, Withe, Shaw, John Gregory and Graham Taylor among the many

he has mentioned throughout the course of his 17 novels. Although Lee is based in New York, he grew up in Handsworth Wood – and is a lifelong Villa fan. His all-time favourite Villa player is Gordon Cowans, who helped the club to the League Championship in 1981 and the European Cup the following year.

MCGRATH THE POP STAR!

Villa legend Paul McGrath embarked on a new career at the age of 52 – as a pop star!

The former Republic of Ireland defender, regarded by many as Villa's greatest-ever player, recorded an album entitled *Handle With Care*, with some of the proceeds going to charity.

WHOSE SHIRT
IS IT?

The names are on the shirts but someone has jumbled up the letters.
Can you unscramble them to reveal the Villa players?

1 PRO VET
a: ....

2 ED NUN
a: ....

3 READ NIL
a: ....

4 OZ-IN-BAG
a: ....

5 WINE MAN
a: ....

6 DREG RAN
a: ....

7 HAIL JC
a: ....

8 RANK COW
a: ....

9 NET B
a: ....

10 A KERB
a: ....

See if you've got you're answers right... turn to page 60 >

THAT'S MY
« HOME »

Villa's players were born in all corners of the globe. See if you can match these 10 players with their home towns and cities. To give you a start, the first one is correct!

1.
Darren Bent

2.
Eric Lichaj

3.
Ciaran Clark

4.
Stephen Ireland

5.
Gary Gardner

6.
Chris Herd

7.
Marc Albrighton

8.
Gabby Agbonlahor

9.
Shay Given

10.
Andreas Weimann

A. LONDON

C. TAMWORTH

B. MELBOURNE

D. LIFFORD

F. VIENNA

E. CHICAGO

H. HARROW

I. CORK

K. BIRMINGHAM

J. SOLIHULL

See if you've got you're answers right…turn to page 60 >

38

GARDNER

LEARNING ABOUT VILLA

School can be a lot of fun, particularly when all the lessons are about your favourite football team! Here's your time-table for today:

HISTORY

• One hundred years ago Villa won the FA Cup, beating Sunderland 1-0 in the 1913 final - and the victory resulted in a house in County Durham being named after our club.

Sunderland supporter Albert Gillett was so confident his favourite team would lift the Cup that he publicly declared his new home would be named after the winners.

Although Tommy Barber's goal gave Villa victory, Albert was as good as his word!

• Villa are one of the oldest football clubs in the country, having been formed way back in 1874.

• The club were founder members of the Football League in 1888, and have won the FA Cup seven times, the League Championship seven times and the League Cup five times.

• They also won the European Cup in 1982 and the European Super Cup the following year.

MATHS

• Based on last season's squad numbers, if you add Alan Hutton and Charles N'Zogbia you get Marc Albrighton. Or, to put it another way, 2 + 10 = 12!

 +  =

• When Barcelona's Lionel Messi scored 50 goals in Spain's La Liga last season, he broke a record which had been held by a Villa player for more than 80 years. Before Messi's incredible feat, the highest number of goals scored by a player in a European league was 49 by Tom "Pongo" Waring in 1930-31.

ENGLISH

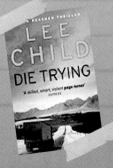

The club have featured in the words of numerous songs and poems over the years - and thriller writer Lee Child's novels are littered with Villa names. One of Lee's books, Die Trying even includes a conversation about the 1982 European Cup final - during a kidnap!

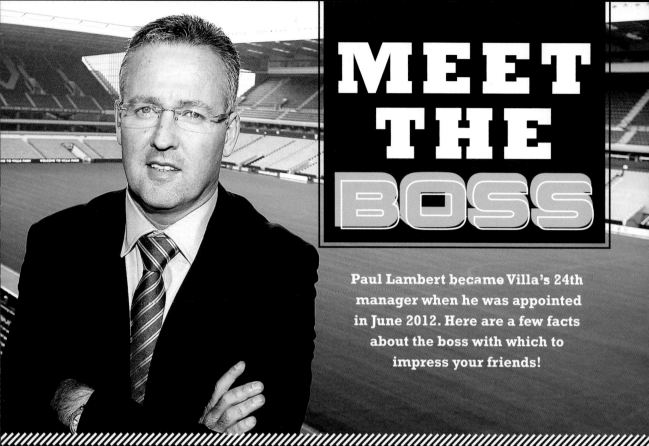

MEET THE BOSS

Paul Lambert became Villa's 24th manager when he was appointed in June 2012. Here are a few facts about the boss with which to impress your friends!

• Paul Christopher Lambert was born on 7th August 1969 in Linwood, Scotland. He started his professional football career with St Mirren in 1985 and at the age of 17 won his first medal when Saints beat Dundee United in the 1987 Scottish Cup final.

• On the day before his 19th birthday, Lambert lined up for a friendly game – against Villa! It was played at St Mirren's old Love Street ground in August 1988 as part of Villa's pre-season trip to Scotland. St Mirren won 1-0.

• Lambert moved to Motherwell in 1993 and helped them finish runners-up in the Scottish Premier League in 1994-95.

• In 1997 he was a member of the Borussia Dortmund team who won the UEFA Champions League, producing an outstanding performance in the German club's 3-1 final victory over Italian giants Juventus.

• During his time with Celtic, the Glasgow club won the Scottish Premier League four times, the Scottish Cup three times and the Scottish League Cup twice.

• He guided the Norwich City to promotion from League One and the Championship in consecutive seasons.

• He was a team-mate of Stiliyan Petrov at Parkhead, and the duo were in the Celtic team, managed by Martin O'Neill, who lost 3-2 to Porto in the 2003 UEFA Cup final in Munich.

• His managerial career started with Livingston in 2005 and he was subsequently in charge of Wycombe Wanderers and Colchester United before taking over at Norwich City.

• Lambert, who was capped 40 times by his country, is Villa's seventh Scottish manager, following in the footsteps of Jimmy McMullan, Alex Massie, George Martin, Tommy Docherty, Billy McNeill and Alex McLeish.

• He is the third manager to have been in charge of both Villa and Norwich on a permanent basis. The others are Ron Saunders and Martin O'Neill, while former Villa striker John Deehan managed Norwich and later had a two-match spell as Villa's caretaker boss, in between Graham Taylor and David O'Leary.

• Lambert has a sharp sense of humour. On the day he was introduced to the media at Villa Park, one reporter asked him: "Did you realise Villa sold 1,000 season tickets when your appointment was announced?" He replied: "Yes, I bought them all!"

FAMOUS FACES

Can you name these famous Villa stars from the past? If you're not sure, Dad should be able to help!

 **1**

 **2**

 **3**

 **4**

 **5**

a: ....

a: ....

a: ....

a: ....

a: ....

DO YOU KNOW SHAY GIVEN...

1. Which club did Shay play for before he joined Villa?

a: ....

2. In which year did he sign for us?

a: ....

3. What is his squad number?

a: ....

4. Which country does he play for?

a: ....

5. Which club did he help to promotion while on loan?

a: ....

Check your answers - turn to page 60 >

LET'S FACE IT

We've incorporated three Villa players into one head. Can you identify them?

Hair
a: ....

Eyes
a: ....

Mouth
a: ....

SPOT THE DIFFERENCE

There are five differences between these two pictures.
Can you spot where they are? Check page 60 for answers (no cheating!).

#1

#2

IRELAND

7

WHO AM I?

How well do you know Villa's stars? Find out by trying to identify these six players from the clues about them. Award yourself three points if you guess correctly on clue A, two if you get it after clue B and one if you need to use clue C. Try testing your knowledge against your friends – but no sneaking a look at the answers!

#1

A I was born in the Republic of Ireland

B I made my Villa debut at Fulham on the opening day of the 2011-12 season

C My previous clubs include Newcastle Utd and Manchester City

a: ....

#2

A My home city is renowned for classical music

B My parents were both champion athletes

C My first Villa goal gave the team a dramatic late win at home to Fulham

a: ....

#3

A I was born in Ireland in 1990

B I joined Villa in January 2012 after signing a pre-contract agreement a few months earlier

C I played for my previous club Shamrock Rovers in the Europa League

a: ....

#4

A I can play either in midfield or as a full-back

B My first goal for Villa was in front of Liverpool's famous Kop

C I was born in Melbourne, Australia

a: ....

#5

A My Villa debut was away to Chelsea on New Year's Eve 2011

B My older brother also played for Villa

C I'm one of six brothers – but only three of us are Villa fans!

a: ....

#6

A I was born in northern France

B My first English club were Newcastle United

C I joined Villa from Wigan Athletic

a: ....

Finished? Check your answers! Turn to page 60 >

DARREN'S
« TOP 10 »

Darren Bent missed a huge chunk of the 2011-12 campaign after suffering a serious ankle injury in February but he still headed Villa's goal chart with 10 – nine in the Premier League and one in the FA Cup. Here's the lowdown on Darren's Top 10:

1 BLACKBURN ROVERS (h) 3-1

A 30-yard shot from Stiliyan Petrov hits defender Grant Hanley just inside the penalty area, and Darren controls the ball before lashing a left-foot shot past keeper Paul Robinson.

2 WIGAN ATHLETIC (h) 2-0

Darren's first goal for Villa at the Holte End – a right-foot volley into the bottom corner from six yards following Gabby Agbonlahor's perfect cross from the left.

3 WEST BROMWICH ALBION (h) 1-2

Ben Foster has no chance as deadly Darren hammers home a powerful penalty after Agbonlahor is brought down by the Albion keeper in the 23rd minute.

4 NORWICH CITY (h) 3-2

The England international provides a clinical finish after Agbonlahor accepts Stephen Warnock's short pass and slips past Kyle Naughton to deliver a superb low centre.

NORWICH CITY (h) 3-2

Darren's second goal against the Canaries is again set up by Agbonlahor, who crosses for his fellow striker to cleverly divert the ball past keeper John Ruddy with the outside of his right boot.

CHELSEA (a) 3-1

Going on as a late sub at Stamford Bridge, Darren calmly slips the ball past Petr Cech after Stephen Ireland intercepts Frank Lampard's pass and darts through the middle to create an inviting chance.

EVERTON (h) 1-1

Holding off a challenge from defender Phil Neville, Villa's record signing forces the ball into the net from close range after Ireland knocks it across the goalmouth.

WOLVES (a) 3-2

Darren calmly sends keeper Wayne Hennessy the wrong way from the penalty spot after being brought down by Christophe Berra at Molineux.

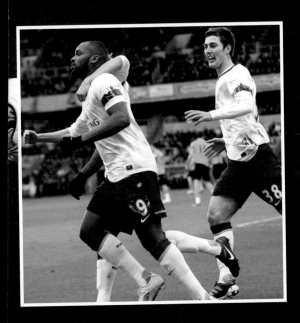

ARSENAL (a) 2-3

His initial shot is turned away by Lukasz Fabianski but Darren reacts smartly to stroke home a low shot from an acute angle in a fourth-round FA Cup-tie at the Emirates Stadium.

QPR (h) 2-2

It's a very special goal for Darren – his 100th in the Premier League – as he gets in front of his marker to slot home Alan Hutton's low centre from the right.

47

MASCOT MANIA

So you want to be a Villa match-day mascot at Villa Park? The only way to do it is to become a member of JV-Life, the club's fantastic junior club for youngsters aged 14 and under.

As you can see from our photo - taken on the final day of last season - those lucky enough to be randomly selected from JV-Life's membership get to walk out with the players before the match and line up for the handshakes before kick-off.

You could be a match-day mascot too!

What else does it include?

The mascot package also includes the chance to practise your skills on the famous Villa Park pitch as well as meeting the players in the tunnel and having a souvenir photo taken with one of your favourite players.

JV-Life is fronted by Villa's mascots, Hercules, Bella and Chip, and there are two levels of membership – a free online e-membership and a full membership, which offers you some amazing gifts.

Full JV-Life members receive some great offers in the post, and there are also some brilliant benefits.

THE ULTIMATE FOOTY COMIC FOR ALL JUNIOR MEMBERS

JV LIFE

ISSUE NO 7

PRICE £2.00

I'M ABSEILING DOWN FORT DUNLOP FOR THE ACORNS CHILDRENS HOSPICE APPEAL... WHAT WILL YOU BE DOING?

FEATURING CHIP THE CLUB REPORTER CHECKS OUT OUR LATEST SIGNINGS...

Free sunnies with JV-Life!

New members receive the following items in a welcome pack:

- A welcome letter from Hercules
- An official JV-Life certificate
- Exclusive JV-Life sunglasses (as seen in photo)
- A membership card
- A copy of the JV-Life comic, which is published four times a season

Members also receive a birthday card and Christmas card from our three superheroes – plus invites to exclusive JV-Life parties where you may get to meet some of the players.

Your membership card entitles you to **10% off merchandise** in the club shop plus **10% off certain Villa events** and a **FREE stadium tour.**

All this costs **just £19.95 for a whole year** – and junior season ticket holders receive complimentary membership!

Colour in Chip!

Free online membership meanwhile is open to all children aged 14 or under. By signing up online, you get the chance to play online games, learn about living a healthy lifestyle and build your own superhero to compete in the JV-Life Super League. To check out all the fun...

VISIT JVLIFE.CO.UK

IT'S A FACT

Fascinating facts and figures about the 2011-12 season

MARC'S MILESTONE GOAL

20,000th GOAL!

Marc Albrighton was a winner when Villa faced Arsenal at home just before Christmas even though the team lost 2-1.

The winger's 54th-minute equaliser against the Gunners was the 20,000th goal to be scored in the Premier League since its inception in 1992.

And as a result of Marc's milestone goal, the club's charity partners, Acorns, received a cheque for £20,000.

"It was great to have that achievement on my shoulders," said Marc, who was just two when Brian Deane scored the first Premier League goal for Sheffield United against Manchester United in August 1992.

TON-UP DARREN  100

COME IN NUMBER 9

The season ended early for Darren Bent when he was injured at Wigan in February. But at least he finally got to wear the No.9 shirt made famous by Villa strikers such as Andy Gray, Peter Withe, Dean Saunders, Dion Dublin and Juan Pablo Angel.

"It's the first time in my career I've had this number," said the England international. "At Ipswich I was 18, at Charlton it was 10, with Spurs I was 23 then 10 and at Sunderland it was 11. Then I was 39 for my first few months with Villa but I've always wanted to be number nine."

Darren Bent scored his 100th Premier League goal when he was on target just before half-time in the 2-2 draw against QPR at Villa Park.

And the club's record signing spelled it out in footballs as he later posed for a special photo to mark the achievement.

Darren, who scored his first Premier goal for Ipswich Town against Middlesbrough in 2002, said it was "fantastic" to reach his century in a Villa shirt.

CHRIS
TAKES IT AS

1ST FOR 6

Six players netted their first Villa goal during the course of the season. Eric Lichaj led the way in the 2-0 Carling Cup victory over Hereford United and was followed by Stephen Ireland (v Chelsea), Robbie Keane (v Wolves), Charles N'Zogbia (v QPR), Andreas Weimann (v Fulham) and Chris Herd (v Liverpool).

Not many footballers are voted man-of-the-match after being sent off - but it happened to Chris Herd.

The Australian midfielder received 34.5 per cent of votes from supporters for his display in the 2-1 home defeat by West Bromwich Albion, despite being shown a red card in the 34th minute. The red card was later rescinded when the FA ruled the decision had been too harsh.

McGREGOR'S THE MAN

Exactly 100 years after his death in December 1911, William McGregor's grave at St Mary's Church, Handsworth, was re-dedicated following a special service of tribute to the former Villa chairman and founder of the Football League.

ROTTERDAM REMEMBERED

Nearly 30 years after their triumph over Bayern Munich in Rotterdam, Villa's 1982 European Cup-winning squad were inducted into the National Football Museum's Hall of Fame, with former manager Ron Saunders performing the ceremony.

STEPHEN'S LUCKY 7

101 SEASONS, 749 PLAYERS

The 2011-12 campaign was Villa's 101st in English football's top flight and by the end of the season 749 players had represented the club in either the First Division or the Premier League. The seven debut boys last season were Shay Given, Charles N'Zogbia, Alan Hutton, Jermaine Jenas, Gary Gardner, Robbie Keane and Samir Carruthers

With Darren Bent being handed the No 9 shirt, Stephen Ireland switched to No 7 at the start of the season - and that suited him just fine.

"Seven has always been my number," said the Irish midfielder. "As a kid I was a big fan of Manchester United's Eric Cantona and that's what he wore."

SPOT THE « BALL »

Using your skill and knowledge, can you locate the ball in this picture?

	A	B	C	D	E	F	G
1							
2							
3							
4							
5							

PLAYERS & MANAGERS

The surnames of the Super Six appear in this word search. Can you find them?

```
A  T  L  I  T  T  L  E
T  M  A  S  S  I  E  M
K  W  H  C  V  N  L  S
I  B  S  R  Q  U  F  T
N  Y  R  O  G  E  R  G
S  R  O  W  E  J  D  E
O  T  V  E  C  K  A  L
N  O  T  H  G  U  O  H
```

Six Villa players have gone on to become manager of the club –

Alex MASSIE

Eric HOUGHTON

Vic CROWE

Ron ATKINSON

Brian LITTLE

John GREGORY

Finished? Check your answers! Turn to page 60 >

AWAY WITH
THE LADS

We all know what to expect when Villa step out for home matches – the players wearing the traditional claret and blue kit which has served the club for well over a century.

But it can be a different story on the road, with Villa often required to switch to different colours to avoid a clash with the home team. In recent years the team have worn a range of different colours on their travels – from white to yellow, from black to grey.

We proudly present the club's various away kits from 2000 right up to the end of last season, courtesy of John Devlin, who has published two volumes of *True Colours*, books which are devoted to football kits. For more information, go to John's website – www.truecoloursfootballkits.com.

2000-01

2001-02

2002-03

2004-05

DWS INVESTMENTS

2005-06

32RED.com ♥♠♦♣

2006-07

acorns

2008-09

32RED.com ♥♦♠♣

2007-08

acorns

2009-10

2010-11

FxPro
Trade Forex Like a Pro

云顶
GENTING
CASINOS

2011-12

55

DESIGN AN

AWAY KIT

Now you've had a look at Villa's away kits over the past 12 seasons, maybe you would like to come up with your own ideas for an away kit – maybe even using totally different colours!

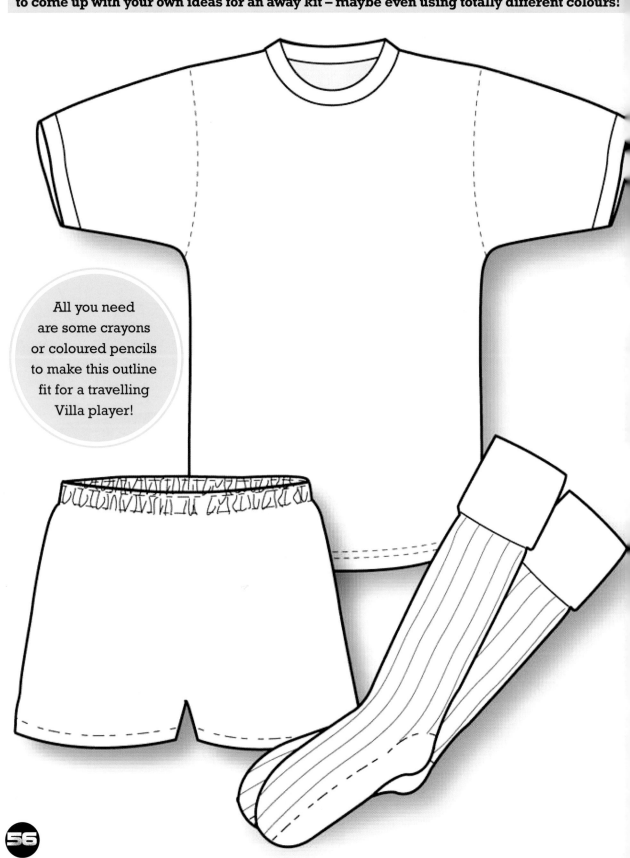

All you need are some crayons or coloured pencils to make this outline fit for a travelling Villa player!

26

WEIMANN

Recipe

CLARETTI SPAGHETTI

You will need:

3 tablespoons of olive oil
1 finely chopped onion
4 finely chopped cloves of garlic
300g of spaghetti or pasta shapes
160g of strong blue cheese, cut into cubes
300g cherry tomatoes
salt and black pepper to taste.

> The players often have a pasta dish before the game, as it gives them the slow-release energy they need to play well. Try it yourself with the help of an adult; it's easy and it's a delicious claret-and-blue meal!

Method:

1 – Heat the oil in a large, non-stick saucepan or frying pan. Add the onion and garlic, and cook on a medium heat until soft, stirring all the time.
2 – Add the tomatoes, and cook on a low heat for 10 minutes.
3 – Cook the pasta in a large pan, adding salt to the water. Drain well.
4 – Put the pasta into the tomato and onion sauce, add the pepper and mix gently. Try not to break the tomatoes too much.
5 – Pour it into a bowl, and sprinkle the cubes of blue cheese all over the top. Serve at once.

ANSWERS

WHOSE SHIRT IS IT? – PAGE 35

1. PETROV
2. DUNNE
3. IRELAND
4. N'ZOGBIA
5. WEIMANN
6. GARDNER
7. LICHAJ
8. WARNOCK
9. BENT
10. BAKER

THAT'S MY HOME – PAGE 36

1A. DARREN BENT (LONDON)
2E. ERIC LICHAJ (CHICAGO)
3H. CIARAN CLARK (HARROW)
4I. STEPHEN IRELAND (CORK)
5J. GARY GARDNER (SOLIHULL)
6B. CHRIS HERD (MELBOURNE)
7C. MARC ALBRIGHTON (TAMWORTH)
8K. GABBY AGBONLAHOR (BIRMINGHAM)
9D. SHAY GIVEN (LIFFORD)
10F. ANDREAS WEIMANN (VIENNA)

FAMOUS FACES – PAGE 40

1. CHICO HAMILTON
2. BRIAN LITTLE
3. GARY SHAW
4. PAUL MCGRATH
5. IAN TAYLOR

DO YOU KNOW SHAY GIVEN? – PAGE 40

1. MANCHESTER CITY
2. 2011
3. NUMBER 1
4. REPUBLIC OF IRELAND
5. SUNDERLAND

LET'S FACE IT – PAGE 40

HAIR – SHAY GIVEN
EYES – ANDREAS WEIMANN
MOUTH – RICHARD DUNNE

SPOT THE DIFFERENCE – PAGE 42

WHO AM I? – PAGE 44

1. SHAY GIVEN
2. ANDREAS WEIMANN
3. ENDA STEVENS
4. CHRIS HERD
5. GARY GARDNER
6. CHARLES N'ZOGBIA

WORDSEARCH – PAGE 52

A	T	L	I	T	T	L	E
T	M	A	S	S	I	E	M
K	W	H	C	V	N	L	S
I	B	S	R	Q	U	F	T
N	Y	R	O	G	E	R	G
S	R	O	W	E	J	D	E
O	T	V	E	C	K	A	L
N	O	T	H	G	U	O	H

SPOT THE BALL – PAGE 52

E5

	A	B	C	D	E	F	G
1							
2							
3							
4							
5